3336 1152

Inside the NFL

THE
CINCINNATI
BENGALS

BOB ITALIA
ABDO & Daughters

Published by Abdo & Daughters, 4940 Viking Drive, Suite 622, Edina, Minnesota 55435.

Printed in the United States.

Cover Photo credits: Wide World Photos/ Allsport
Interior Photo credits: Wide World Photos

Edited by Paul Joseph

Library of Congress Cataloging-in-Publication

Italia, Bob, 1955—
        The Cincinnati Bengals / Bob Italia.
        p.   cm. -- (Inside the NFL).
Includes Index.
Summary: Provides a look at some of the key players in the history of the American Football Conference Cincinnati Bengals.
        ISBN 1-56239-535-1
1. Cincinnati Bengals (Football team) -- History--Juvenile literature. 2. National Football League--History--Juvenile literature. [1. Cincinnati Bengals (football team)--History.]
I. Title. II. Series: Italia, Bob, 1955— Inside the NFL.
GV956.C54I83   1996
796.332'64'0977178--dc20   95-44794
                                                                CIP
                                                                AC

CONTENTS

Almost Great 4

Paul Brown 6

Ken Anderson..8

Reggie Williams 10

The Super Bowl 11

Sam Wyche and Boomer 13

The Ickey Shuffle 17

A Super Return...22

A Slow Decline 24

Shula Arrives 26

Jeff Blake...27

A Long Climb 28

Glossary 29

Index 31

Almost Great

In the early 1980s, the Cincinnati Bengals flirted with greatness. They fielded a strong defense and explosive offense that got them to the Super Bowl in 1981. Though they lost, they seemed ready to dominate their league.

But those Bengals never returned to the Super Bowl. Slowly, that AFC championship team fell apart, until their stars—Ken Anderson, Ross Browner, Isaac Curtis, Pete Johnson, and Cris Collinsworth—had finally retired.

Cris Collinsworth, receiver for the Bengals.

The Bengals returned to the Super Bowl in 1988 with a new team led by quarterback Boomer Esiason. They led the game at the very end—only to lose on a last-minute touchdown. Since that time, the Bengals have been searching for the right combination of players to lead them back to greatness.

With the addition of quarterback Jeff Blake, the Bengals seemed to be on the right track. But they are still in the midst of their biggest slump in franchise history, and it may take a long time for this young team to jell into a playoff contender.

Opposite page: Quarterback Boomer Esiason drops back to throw a pass.

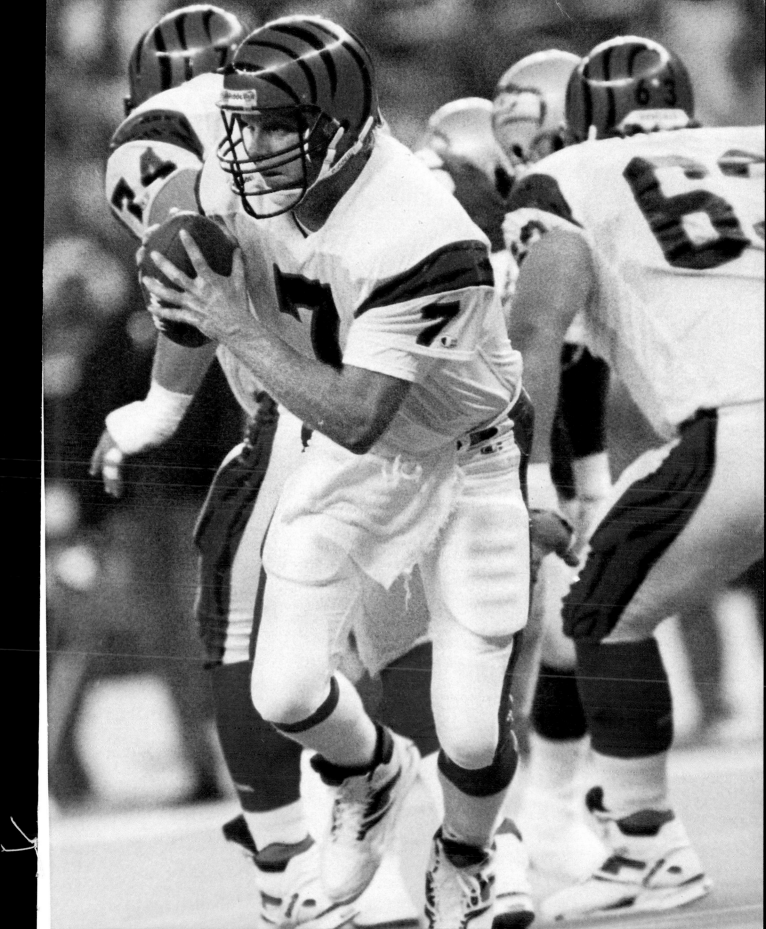

Paul Brown

In 1968, the Cincinnati Bengals began playing in the American Football League (AFL). Paul Brown was the owner, general manager, and head coach. He had built the Cleveland Browns into one of the most successful teams in the history of the National Football League. Brown retired in 1962 from the team he built. When he heard the Bengals were forming, he decided to return to professional football.

The Bengals were made up of rookies and young players who did not fit in with other professional football teams. They weren't winners at first, but they played competitively.

It didn't take long for Brown to mold his team into winners. In only their third year, Cincinnati won the Central Division of the American Football Conference (AFC). (The NFL and the AFL merged in 1970.) However, they lost in the first playoff round to the Baltimore Colts.

The team had young stars such as running back Essex Johnson, middle linebacker Bill Bergey, defensive tackle Mike Reid, and cornerback Lemar Parrish. They formed a solid foundation on which Brown could build a championship team.

Brown needed solid play from his quarterback position. Greg Cook performed well in 1969, but an injury ended his career. Virgil Carter showed promise, but he suffered many injuries throughout his career.

**Opposite page:
Bill Bergey was one of the
Bengals first stars.**

Ken Anderson

Fortunately for Brown, his scouts found a quarterback who had the potential for greatness. His name was Ken Anderson. Anderson was a relatively unknown player from tiny Augustana College. When the Cincinnati scouts told Brown about Anderson, Brown wondered if a young quarterback from a small school could survive the pressures of the NFL. Augustana never had big crowds at their football games. How would Anderson perform in front of tens of thousands of NFL football fans?

Quarterback Ken Anderson fades back to pass.

When Carter suffered another injury, Anderson saw a lot of action during his rookie season. By the following season, Anderson became the Bengals' starting quarterback—a rare feat, considering the fact that Brown rarely played young quarterbacks. But Brown knew Anderson was a unique talent. He compared Anderson with Hall-of-Fame quarterback Otto Graham. While he played, Graham led Cleveland to several championships.

The Bengals won the Central Division title in 1973, but lost in the playoffs to Miami. They returned to the playoffs again in 1975 but were eliminated in the first round by the Oakland Raiders. By then, Anderson had become one of the best passers in the NFL. In a 1974 game against the Pittsburgh Steelers, Anderson was 20-for-22 in passing.

Quarterback Ken Anderson throwing a pass against the Houston Oilers, 1982.

During the mid-1970s, the Bengals often challenged for first place in the AFC Central Division. Besides Anderson, the Bengals had speedy wide receiver Isaac Curtis and giant running back Charles "Boobie" Clark.

On defense, Mike Reid and Sherman White dominated the line of scrimmage. Linebackers Bergey and Jim LeClair were strong against the run and the pass. And Parrish was still playing well at cornerback.

But the Bengals started to fade at the end of the 1970s and eventually fell to last place in the division in 1980. In 1981, the team received new tiger-striped helmets. Suddenly, they found themselves on top of the AFC Central Division. The play of rookie wide receiver Cris Collinsworth and running back Pete Johnson had much to do with the Bengals' dramatic rise to the top. On defense, a new star emerged. His name was Reggie Williams.

Reggie Williams

When Williams was young, he did not dream of becoming a football player. He did not show an interest in sports. Williams wanted to be an outstanding student, and worked hard at it.

There was only one problem: Williams was born partially deaf. Many of his teachers thought Williams was a slow learner. He was placed in a class with children who had learning problems.

When his hearing problem was finally uncovered, Williams returned to regular classes. Several teachers helped him overcome his hearing problem.

When he was in high school, Williams developed an interest in sports. He eventually attended Dartmouth College—one of the top schools in the country. At Dartmouth, Williams developed into an outstanding football player. In 1975, the Bengals drafted him. He played for the Bengals for fifteen years as an outside linebacker.

Williams was a leader on the field. He and fellow linebacker Jim LeClair anchored a defense that helped the Bengals capture the division crown in 1981. Defensive linemen Ross Browner and Eddie Edwards developed into fierce pass rushers. And defensive backs Ken Riley and Louis Breeden played well in the secondary.

The offense was the real story in 1981. Anderson was named AFC Player of the Year. He set team records for most yards passing (3,754 yards) and most touchdowns (29) in a season. Pete Johnson broke the team's single-season rushing record with 1,077 yards and scored a record-16 touchdowns.

In the playoffs, Cincinnati defeated the Buffalo Bills 28-21 at home, then manhandled the San Diego Chargers 27-7 in the AFC Championship game. Cincinnati had won its first Super Bowl berth. Now they would have to face the San Francisco 49ers and Joe Montana.

The Super Bowl

Cincinnati fell behind San Francisco 20-0 at halftime. At the time, it was the most one-sided halftime score in Super Bowl history. But the Bengals came out of the locker room, took the kickoff, and marched 83-yards for a touchdown. They were back in the game.

Anderson continued to rally his team in the second half. Though wide receivers Isaac Curtis and Cris Collinsworth were well-covered, Anderson often found tight end Dan Ross wide open. Ross caught eleven passes—a Super Bowl record— as the Bengals scored 21 second-half points. But San Francisco held on for a 26-21 victory.

Receiver Isaac Curtis (85) on his way to a touchdown.

The Bengals won their division again in 1982 and returned to the playoffs. But they lost to the New York Jets 44-17 in the first round. Williams had his best year ever in 1983, recording 7.5 quarterback sacks and four fumble recoveries. However, the Bengals finished 7-9 and out of the playoffs. After the season, head coach Forrest Gregg took the head coaching job with the Green Bay Packers. It was time to rebuild again.

Cris Collinsworth (80) makes his way down field.

Sam Wyche and Boomer

Former San Francisco quarterback coach Sam Wyche became head coach in 1984. Wyche had played quarterback for the Bengals when the team formed in 1968. Wyche helped develop the skills of San Francisco quarterback Joe Montana. Now he had the chance to work with rookie quarterback Boomer Esiason, who the Bengals picked in the second round of the 1984 draft.

Bengals head coach Sam Wyche.

Bengal quarterback Boomer Esiason passes against the Los Angeles Raiders, 1988.

Esiason played college football at the University of Maryland where he had much success. His real name is Norman, but he earned the name "Boomer" because he kicked in his mother's womb. Boomer had always been a star, but he would struggle in his first few years of pro football.

Anderson's solid play kept Esiason on the bench for a while, but eventually Esiason won the starting quarterback job. As a result, the Bengals showed improvement. In 1986, Esiason led Cincinnati to a 10-6 record. That season, only Dan Marino of the Miami Dolphins threw for more yards in the AFC than Esiason. In addition, James Brooks rushed for 1,087 yards.

In 1987, the NFL Players Association went on strike. The NFL owners used "replacement" players for part of the season. When the "real" players returned, the Bengals did not play well. The team had expected to challenge for the division title. Instead, they finished with a 4-11 record—good for last place.

Management and fans expected much from Esiason and Wyche in 1988. It was a make-or-break season. If the Bengals won, all would be forgiven. But if they lost, Wyche knew he would lose his job. It was time for Esiason to take the Bengals to a higher level of play.

Boomer Esiason scrambles
to make a pass.

The Ickey Shuffle

Wyche knew his team needed to improve its running game. When the 1988 training camp began, rookie fullback Elbert "Ickey" Woods caught Wyche's attention. Woods ran hard—sometimes over some people. Wyche knew he had his running back.

Ever since he was a child, Woods wanted to be a football player. But Woods grew up in a Fresno, California, neighborhood where kids often turn to crime and drugs. To get away from those troubled streets, he earned a scholarship at the University of Nevada-Las Vegas (UNLV). Woods and teammate Andre Horn, also from Fresno, often talked about becoming professional football players.

Running back Ickey Woods scampers past Buffalo defenders.

CINCINNATI
BENGALS

Ken Anderson joins the
team in 1971.

Tim Krumrie becomes a
Bengal in 1983.

20

0

5

CINCIN
BENG

Cris Collinsworth signs
in 1981.

10   20   30   40   5

0   40   20   10

In 1988, Boomer Esiason is named the NFL's Offensive Player of the Year.

NNATI
GALS

CINCINNATI
BENGALS

In 1994, Jeff Blake becomes the starting quarterback.

Sam Wyche leads the Bengals to the Super Bowl in 1988.

0   40   30   20   10

Woods wasn't a star at UNLV until his senior year. Before that time, he had been a backup fullback. When he finally got a chance to start, Woods showed his talents. But by then, his friend Horn wasn't around. He had been shot and killed in Fresno.

It didn't take long for Woods to make the starting lineup. He ran hard, and developed a talent for finding the end zone. Led by Woods and Esiason, the Bengals captured first place in the AFC Central Division.

The Bengals were fun to watch. They had an electrifying passing game and scored often. Woods danced after every touchdown he scored. The Cincinnati news reporters started calling his dance the "Ickey Shuffle."

From left: Lewis Billups, David Fulcher, Ickey Woods, Solomon Wilcots, and Eric Thomas do the "Ickey Shuffle."

Soon, everyone was doing the Ickey Shuffle—including teammates and fans. Even 80-year-old Paul Brown was doing it—and with good reason. In 1988, Woods rushed for 1,066 yards and scored 15 touchdowns. James Brooks ran for 931 yards and scored 8 touchdowns. Offensive linemen Anthony Munoz, Max Montoya, and Joe Walter helped clear the way.

But Esiason was the biggest star. He threw for 3,572 yards and 28 touchdowns. For his efforts Esiason was named the NFL Offensive Player of the Year.

The Bengals' defense also had a great year. Thirty-four-year-old Reggie Williams had one of his best seasons. Tim Krumrie led the team in tackles, and safety David Fulcher played tough against the run. Management and fans were happy again. Sam Wyche and his Bengals could do no wrong.

But the regular-season success only heightened playoff expectations for Cincinnati. Not only did fans expect the Bengals to do well in the postseason, they wanted a Super Bowl championship.

With the team Sam Wyche had assembled and the way they were playing, there was every reason to think that Cincinnati could win it all. The Bengals had home field advantage throughout the AFC playoffs. All they had to do was beat two teams—the Seattle Seahawks and the Buffalo Bills—to earn their second Super Bowl appearance.

Against the Seahawks, Cincinnati jumped out to a 21-0 halftime lead and held on for a 21-13 victory as Woods scored the game-winner on a one-yard run. In the AFC championship game, the defense held Buffalo to 181 total yards—and only 45 yards rushing. Meanwhile, Woods pounded out 102 yards on 29 carries as the Bengals seized a 14-10 halftime lead. Woods' touchdown plunge in the fourth quarter sealed the 21-10 victory. Now it was on to the Super Bowl to face an old nemesis—Joe Montana and the San Francisco 49ers.

A Super Return

San Francisco was the same team that defeated the Bengals in the 1982 Super Bowl. This time, however, Cincinnati was determined to win a world championship.

The first half was a defensive struggle. The Cincinnati offense could not move the ball. But the defense held the 49ers to a lone field goal in the first half. Unfortunately for the Bengals, they lost Krumrie in the first quarter with a broken leg. Despite this loss, the game was tied 3-3 at halftime.

In the second half, the offense started clicking. Esiason led Cincinnati on a 61-yard drive in the third quarter that resulted in a Jim Breech field goal and a 6-3 lead.

San Francisco came back to tie the game late in the third quarter. The tie lasted until the kickoff. Stanford Jennings took the ball at the Bengals' 7-yard line and rambled 93 yards for a touchdown. The Bengals were back on top, 13-6.

But Joe Montana led the 49ers downfield in only four plays from San Francisco's 15-yard line and hit Jerry Rice for the tying touchdown. Cincinnati then drove to the 49ers' 22-yard line where Jim Breech kicked his third field goal, a 40-yarder, to give the Bengals a 16-13 lead with only 3:20 remaining.

But three minutes was too much time to give Joe Montana. He led the 49ers on one last drive and threw the winning touchdown with 34 seconds remaining in the game. All Sam Wyche could do was stand there and watch Montana work his magic. "Thirty-four seconds," Wyche muttered on the sidelines. "We were thirty-four seconds away." San Francisco won 20-16, and the Bengals went home disappointed—but still believing they could become NFL champions the following season.

Bengals nose tackle Tim Krumrie goes up against the Buffalo Bills in the AFC Championship, 1989.

A Slow Decline

In 1989, however, injuries hurt Cincinnati's championship dreams. Ickey Woods missed most of the year after hurting his knee in the second game. Esiason had a sore shoulder that bothered him throughout the season. Krumrie recovered from his broken leg, but he could not dominate the line of scrimmage. Despite the injuries, the Bengals finished 9-7 and nearly made the playoffs. At the end of the season, Reggie Williams retired.

In 1990, the Bengals opened the season by winning three straight games. But they were 4-7 through the next 11 games before winning their final two. A soft defense and an inconsistent passing game prevented the Bengals from dominating the league, even though they did win their division with a 9-7 record. Esiason threw 24 touchdowns but had 22 interceptions. Woods rebounded from his injury, but James Brooks stole the show with another 1,000-yard season.

In the first round of the playoffs, Cincinnati trounced the Houston Oilers 41-14. The Bengals jumped out to a 20-0 halftime lead and never looked back. It was 34-0 in the third quarter before Houston scored its first points. It looked as though the Bengals had finally hit their stride.

But in the second round, the Bengals had to play the Raiders in Los Angeles. This time, the game was much closer. The Raiders took a 7-3 halftime lead, then added a third quarter field goal. The Bengals tied the game on an 8-yard touchdown pass from Esiason to Jennings. But Los Angeles scored ten unanswered points for a 20-10 win.

Opposite page:
James Brooks (21) runs through the Seahawks defense.

Shula Arrives

The Bengals still had high hopes for the 1991 season. But Cincinnati lost its first eight games and finished 3-13. After the season, Wyche was replaced by 32-year-old Dave Shula, son of Miami coach Don Shula. Dave became the youngest head coach in modern NFL history.

Shula started 2-0 in 1992. But the team finished with back-to-back 10-loss seasons for the first time in over a decade. Esiason finished as a backup to rookie David Klingler. Another era ended when tackle Anthony Munoz announced his retirement following 13 seasons of dominating line play. Harold Green had 1,170 yards rushing and nose tackle Tim Krumrie led the defense with 97 tackles. Rookies Carl Pickens, Darryl Williams and Ricardo McDonald were also impressive. But the Bengals still had a lot of rebuilding to do.

That became apparent in 1993 when the team lost its first 10 games. Even though the Bengals won three of its final six games, their 3-13 mark tied for the worst team record. Cincinnati got rid of most of its high-priced veterans before the start of the season, and the inexperience showed. Their 16-game total of 187 points was a record-low for the franchise. Klingler showed improvement, but like the team, he had a long way to go.

Jeff Blake

In 1994, Esiason was traded to the New York Jets. Cincinnati lost their opener 28-20 to the Cleveland Browns—and it was all downhill from there. By Week 9, they were 0-8. But they played the Dallas Cowboys tough, losing only 23-20. Finally, they looked as though they were turning the corner.

In Week 9, they got their first victory. With 6:46 left in overtime, Doug Pelfrey kicked his sixth field goal of the game—a team record—and the Bengals surprised Seattle 20-17. Rookie quarterback Jeff Blake set up the winning kick with a 76-yard pass to fellow rookie Darnay Scott, who carried it to the Seattle 7-yard line. Blake passed for 387 yards in his second start.

The trend continued the following week with a 34-31 win over the Houston Oilers. But then five more losses in a row dropped their record to 2-13. A season-ending 33-30 win over the Eagles gave the Bengals their second 3-13 record in a row.

Jeff Blake takes over at quarterback for Esiason.

A Long Climb

With Jeff Blake at quarterback, the Bengals seem to have their a talented signal-caller in place. But to be competitive, Cincinnati needs to surround him with solid offensive players. The defense also needs vast improvement.

The Bengals are young, and so too is their head coach. If management exercises patience and allows the team to develop, Cincinnati may find themselves on the road to the playoffs.

Quarterback Jeff Blake looks for a receiver against the Seahawks, 1994.

GLOSSARY

ALL-PRO—A player who is voted to the Pro Bowl.

BACKFIELD—Players whose position is behind the line of scrimmage.

CORNERBACK—Either of two defensive halfbacks stationed a short distance behind the linebackers and relatively near the sidelines.

DEFENSIVE END—A defensive player who plays on the end of the line and often next to the defensive tackle.

DEFENSIVE TACKLE—A defensive player who plays on the line and between the guard and end.

ELIGIBLE—A player who is qualified to be voted into the Hall of Fame.

END ZONE—The area on either end of a football field where players score touchdowns.

EXTRA POINT—The additional one-point score added after a player makes a touchdown. Teams earn extra points if the placekicker kicks the ball through the uprights of the goalpost, or if an offensive player crosses the goal line with the football before being tackled.

FIELD GOAL—A three-point score awarded when a placekicker kicks the ball through the uprights of the goalpost.

FULLBACK—An offensive player who often lines up farthest behind the front line.

FUMBLE—When a player loses control of the football.

GUARD—An offensive lineman who plays between the tackles and center.

GROUND GAME—The running game.

HALFBACK—An offensive player whose position is behind the line of scrimmage.

HALFTIME—The time period between the second and third quarters of a football game.

INTERCEPTION—When a defensive player catches a pass from an offensive player.

KICK RETURNER—An offensive player who returns kickoffs.

LINEBACKER—A defensive player whose position is behind the line of scrimmage.

LINEMAN—An offensive or defensive player who plays on the line of scrimmage.

PASS—To throw the ball.

PASS RECEIVER—An offensive player who runs pass routes and catches passes.

PLACEKICKER—An offensive player who kicks extra points and field goals. The placekicker also kicks the ball from a tee to the opponent after his team has scored.

PLAYOFFS—The postseason games played amongst the division winners and wild card teams which determines the Super Bowl champion.

PRO BOWL—The postseason All-Star game which showcases the NFL's best players.

PUNT—To kick the ball to the opponent.

QUARTER—One of four 15-minute time periods that makes up a football game.

QUARTERBACK—The backfield player who usually calls the signals for the plays.

REGULAR SEASON—The games played after the preseason and before the playoffs.

ROOKIE—A first-year player.

RUNNING BACK—A backfield player who usually runs with the ball.

RUSH—To run with the football.

SACK—To tackle the quarterback behind the line of scrimmage.

SAFETY—A defensive back who plays behind the linemen and linebackers. Also, two points awarded for tackling an offensive player in his own end zone when he's carrying the ball.

SPECIAL TEAMS—Squads of football players that perform special tasks (for example, kickoff team and punt-return team).

SPONSOR—A person or company that finances a football team.

SUPER BOWL—The NFL Championship game played between the AFC champion and the NFC champion.

T FORMATION—An offensive formation in which the fullback lines up behind the center and quarterback with one halfback stationed on each side of the fullback.

TACKLE—An offensive or defensive lineman who plays between the ends and the guards.

TAILBACK—The offensive back farthest from the line of scrimmage.

TIGHT END—An offensive lineman who is stationed next to the tackles, and who usually blocks or catches passes.

TOUCHDOWN—When one team crosses the goal line of the other team's end zone. A touchdown is worth six points.

TURNOVER—To turn the ball over to an opponent either by a fumble, an interception, or on downs.

UNDERDOG—The team that is picked to lose the game.

WIDE RECEIVER—An offensive player who is stationed relatively close to the sidelines and who usually catches passes.

WILD CARD—A team that makes the playoffs without winning its division.

ZONE PASS DEFENSE—A pass defense method where defensive backs defend a certain area of the playing field rather than individual pass receivers.

INDEX

A

AFC championship 4
Anderson, Ken 4, 8, 9, 10, 11, 15
Augustana College 8

B

Baltimore Colts 6
Bergey, Bill 6, 9
Blake, Jeff 4, 27, 28
Breeden, Louis 10
Brown, Paul 6, 8, 9, 21
Browner, Ross 4, 10
Buffalo Bills 10, 21

C

Carter, Virgil 6, 9
Central Division 9, 20
championships 4, 6, 9, 10, 21, 22,
    24
Clark, Charles "Boobie" 9
Cleveland Browns 6, 9, 27
Collinsworth, Cris 4, 9, 11
Cook, Greg 6
Curtis, Isaac 4, 9, 11

D

Dallas Cowboys 27
Dartmouth College 10

E

Edwards, Eddie 10
Esiason, Boomer 4, 13, 15, 20,
    21, 22, 24, 26, 27

F

Fresno (CA) 17, 20

G

Graham, Otto 9
Green Bay Packers 12
Green, Harold 26
Gregg, Forrest 12

H

Horn, Andre 17, 20
Houston Oilers 24, 27

I

"Ickey Shuffle" 20, 21

J

Johnson, Essex 6
Johnson, Pete 4, 9, 10

K

Klingler, David 26
Krumrie, Tim 21, 22, 24, 26

L

Los Angeles Raiders 24

M

Marino, Dan 15
McDonald, Ricardo 26
Montana, Joe 13, 21, 22
Munoz, Anthony 21, 26

N

National Football League (NFL) 6
New York Jets 12, 27

P

Parrish, Lemar 6, 9
Pelfrey, Doug 27
Pickens, Carl 26
Pittsburgh Steelers 9
Player of the Year 10, 21
Players Association 15
players strike 15
playoffs 4, 6, 9, 10, 12, 21, 24, 28

R

Reid, Mike 6, 9
Rice, Jerry 22
Riley, Ken 10
Ross, Dan 11

S

San Diego Chargers 10
San Francisco 49ers 10, 11, 13, 21, 22
Scott, Darnay 27
Seattle Seahawks 21, 27
Shula, Dave 26
Shula, Don 26
Super Bowl 4, 11, 22

U

University of Maryland 15
University of Nevada-Las Vegas (UNLV) 17

W

Williams, Reggie 9, 10, 12, 21, 24
Williams, Darryl 26
Woods, Elbert "Ickey" 17, 20, 21, 24
Wyche, Sam 13, 15, 17, 21, 22, 26